Transform Interests Into Jobs

A Career Practitioner's Guide

Carol Christen & Robin Roman Wright

Carol Christen

parachute4teens.com

Robin Roman Wright

youthleadershipcareers.com

This workbook is for high school guidance counselors,
coaches, career coaches, career counselors,
and college career center counselors

ACKNOWLEDGMENTS

Holly Simpson Eubanks

Copy Editor

linkedin.com/pub/holly-eubanks/30/b32/407/en

Margaret Starvish

Writer/Editor

linkedin.com/in/maggiestarvish

Claire Casaregola

Publication & Cover Art Design

clairecas.com

Printed by CreateSpace, An Amazon.com Company

First Edition: September 2015

Leadership and Careers Press

ISBN-13: 978-0692497302

ISBN-10: 0692497307

Table of Contents

Introduction:

Workbook Purpose:

This workbook is a supplement for professional career counselors and coaches. It provides easy to use exercises to make Career Planning A La Parachute (as described in What Color Is Your Parachute? For Teens and on each of the author's web sites) come alive for your students and/or clients. It includes directions for practitioners and reproducible worksheets for clients, workshop participants or students. The topics in this workbook revolve around helping students/clients translate interests into job targets. Career Practitioners say this step is the most difficult part of the career choice process. We developed this guidebook after surveying readers of our e-zine. Translating interests into job targets was the resource coaches, teachers and counselors most desired.

Completing the activities in this book will enable your students or clients to more intentionally choose job targets or career goals that match their picture of an ideal job. Perhaps even more important, these activities will help teens and young adults create the kind of life that they envision for themselves. The focus is on both self-understanding and gaining knowledge about the job market.

Intended Audience:

Transform Interests Into Jobs, A Career Practitioner's Guide is intended to assist Career Practitioners who work with 11th and 12th grade high school students, 1st and 2nd year college students, and older teens and young adults who are not in college.

The material is designed to be used with individuals for one-on-one coaching or counseling as well as with small groups. The instructions and worksheets can also easily be used by guidance counselors and college career counselors who are teaching career development classes.

In writing *Transform Interests Into Jobs, A Career Practitioner's Guide* we use the term "Career Practitioner" to encompass a broad group of professionals who work with teens and young adults. This can include, but is not limited to, high school guidance counselors, coaches, career coaches, career counselors, and college career center counselors.

Introduction:

Use of Materials:

We ask that you please respect the intellectual property rights of the authors. The materials in this document are licensed to the individual professional or user who purchased this book. The material is licensed for the use of the purchaser alone. Reproducible worksheets on pages 5 – 23 are to be used with the purchaser's own clients, groups or classes.

The purchaser can request a downloadable copy of the reproducible worksheets by submitting a request on http://www.youthleadershipcareers.com/transformreproducibles.

These materials may not be reproduced or presented in any public or private professional presentation without the express written permission of Robin Roman Wright Consulting.

For further information, comments, or suggestions for the improvement of these materials, please contact Robin Roman Wright at
www.youthleadershipcareers.com or
coachrobin@leadershipandcareers.com.

Background

Career Planning A La Parachute:
A Quick Summary:

> The Parachute model of career decision making is divided into categories of
>
> **1** **What**   **2** **Where**   **3** **How**

1 **What** are my skills?

2 **Where** can I use my best skills?

3 **How** will I get a job using my best skills?

1 **What are my skills?** Focuses on skill identification and discernment.*

2 **"Where will I use my best skills?"** Completing the other categories of the Parachute diagram provides answers to the Where question. (See sections of the Parachute For Teens Diagram in Appendix B.) In our current economic environment, finding or creating options in the workplace for earning a living is as important as knowing one's transferable skills.

3 **"How will I get a job that uses my skills and matches me well?"** Practice field surveys, information interviews, and hiring interviews all help answer the How question, while at the same time helping students/clients build a network of like-minded colleagues. Identifying educational requirements is also a key aspect of this part of the process.

Each piece in the process needs the other to achieve the maximum result. Skill identification helps job seekers confirm their favorite skills. Learning where those skills can be used comes from understanding yourself, completing the Parachute Diagram and researching the realities of the job market.

If your students or clients haven't identified their interests, we offer you the exercises on the following two pages to help them do so.

*This workbook will help students and clients answer both the "Where" and the "How" questions. We recommend that students also answer the "What" question as part of the overall Career Planning process. While highly recommended, identification of a student's transferable skill set is not necessary prior to completing the exercises in this workbook. The process for identifying a student or client's transferable skill set is explained in the book *What Color Is Your Parachute? For Teens.* Alternatively, you may have other approaches for skill assessment.

IV

Optional Preliminary Exercise: Identifying Career Interests

We assume your students/clients will have identified their interests prior to completing the set of exercises in this workbook. If your students/clients haven't identified their interests, the following exercises will help them do so.

Exploring Interests:

OBJECTIVES

1 Have students/clients identify 5 interests.

2 Have students/clients generate a list of 15 job titles that are linked to their interests.

Student Exercises

A. Compile a list of at least 5 interests by answering a few of the questions below:

1 In your free time, what do you like to do?

2 What are your hobbies? (Note: Many hobbies–star gazing, fishing, sewing, etc. – are also industries, so if you identify your favorite hobby, you may also have picked a favorite field.)

3 If you could make a movie or YouTube video on any subject, what would that subject be?

4 When friends come to you for help with problems or questions, what are the kinds of problems or questions for which they seek your advice?

5 If some really generous relative gave you a $250 gift certificate to your favorite bookstore, what books would you buy?

B. Come up with 3 jobs that involve each of your top 5 favorite interests. You want to generate a wide range of options. Here are two examples:

1 If you answered "Golf" in A above, what are some different jobs that involve golf?

2 If one of your favorite hobbies is making jewelry, what are some jobs in the field of jewelry manufacturing?

Identifying Career Interests:

OBJECTIVES

1 Have students/clients link jobs titles to job categories.

2 Have students/clients expand their list of possible job titles within areas of interest.

Student Exercises

A For each job title you identified in B on previous page, in what job category would you find this kind of work? Make a list of those job categories. ***Refer to list of Job Categories in Appendix A.***

B Looking at the Job Categories you just listed, identify 3 additional jobs that come to mind that weren't on your original list. ***These might be jobs that you know very little about but they sound interesting and you'd like to learn more about them.***

C Take the Self-Directed-Search or SDS online. This low-cost assessment by PAR, Inc. takes only 20-30 minutes to complete ***http://www.self-directed-search.com/***. By completing this exercise students/clients will identify their Holland Code or Interest Code as noted on O*NET.

D Take a look at:

1. The list of interests from exercise A under "Exploring Interests" on previous page.

2. The list of 15 job titles from exercise B under "Exploring Interests" on previous page.

3. The 3 additional jobs from exercise B under "Identifying Career Interests" on this page.

4. The jobs titles (Occupations) suggested for you from the Self-Directed-Search Client Interpretive Report.

E Review the four lists, mentioned in D above, and circle 5 job titles that most interest you. That is, are you willing to study the subject matter you need to know to be successful in this type of work? Do you have or want to learn the skills needed to do this type of work? List the names of these 5 job titles on the charts provided on pages 6 and 7.

Work Options Research

OBJECTIVES

1. Have students/clients learn key information about 5 jobs that the student is interested in.

2. Have students/clients review their assumptions against real world data in order to choose 3 job targets.

3. Have students/clients rate each position that they learn about as a result of Informational Interviews.

4. Have students/clients identify job characteristics that would be more to their liking.

Student Exercises:

A. Investigate 5 Job Possibilities (pages 5-7)

Use the Internet to investigate the 5 jobs that you have identified a interesting to you. You want to find out the major facts about each of these jobs. The worksheets ask you to learn the following about each one:

1. Official Job Title

2. Common Work Tasks

3. Basic Salary Information

4. Transferable Skills Needed/Used

5. Technical Proficiencies Needed

6. Education or Training – What kind?
   How long is it? How much will it cost?

7. Typical Work Environment

8. Holland Code Matches

*indicates accompanying worksheet

Practitioner's Instructions

B. Choose 3 Job Targets (pages 8-12)

Pick 3 of the job titles that still grab your interest after doing this initial research. (The research is necessary because you want to test your assumptions and the common statements made about this job, or line of work, against information from those who do the work that interests you.)

1   ***Online investigation*** - On page 9: Conduct research on YouTube. List links to at least 1 video about this line of work, field, job or industry. (Watching 2 videos on each job is even better.) Write a sentence about what additional facts you have gathered from the video.

2   ***Online investigation*** - On page 10 & 11: Conduct research on the web using the internet resources listed on page 12.

     A   Identify two professional organizations for each of the 3 jobs that most interest you.

         i   Select one article or web page from the professional organization that describes this job in more detail.

         ii   Write one or two sentences about what additional information you gathered about this job.

C. Field Research & Information Interviews (Pages 13-17)

1   Conduct 3 Information Interviews on each of these jobs. Use instructions and the list of Information Interview questions provided.

2   Record contact information and what you learn from each interview. Use worksheets on pages 16 and 17.

       Note: Career Practitioners need to make 1 additional copy of pages 16 and 17 for each informational interview that students or clients conduct.

3   Use the Job Meter on page 17 to evaluate each job.

Developing An Action Plan:
Career Goal Setting

OBJECTIVES

1. Have students/clients compile summary data on each of the job titles that they have investigated.

2. Have students/clients refine their list of their top 3 job titles based on information learned.

3. Have students/clients write an action plan to continue research so that they can choose one job target to pursue in 3 to 6 months. (This is not to limit students/clients from changing their minds. It is to provide direction for choosing courses in high school and/or college that will enable them to reach a well thought out goal after completing their education.)

4. Have students/clients fill in the Parachute Diagram. (If, addition to this workbook, you are using your own set of career exploration activities then help students translate their discoveries from those exercises into the Parachute categories.)

Student Exercises:

A. Summarize & Rank the 3 Initial Job Titles (pages 18-22)

Review the data you gathered on pages 5 - 17. Complete a 2-page summary for each of the 3 job titles that are still on your list. Then decide if you are still interested in these jobs. Ask yourself, "Since concluding my research, does my interest in this job remain high?" If you answer "Yes," then you are saying you could, and would like to, learn the skills and knowledge to be good at this job. If your answer is no, try to identify another job title. This could be a slightly different job title than the one you first identified, an offshoot of the original, or something you learned about during your research that wasn't on your original list. (You should identify at least two job titles before moving on to the Action Plan.)

> Note: Career Practitioners need to make 2 additional copy of pages 19 and 20 so that each student/client has 3 separate copies of these worksheets.

B. Write An Action Plan (pages 21-23)

1 Write an action plan for how you will learn more about each of the 3 Job Titles in the next three months. Here are some ideas:

- **i** Conduct additional Information Interviews
- **ii** Attend some local professional association meetings
- **iii** Shadow someone in each of your target jobs
- **iv** Obtain an unpaid or paid internship
- **v** Take a class on the subject

2 Identify a list of people who might mentor you or help you as you set about to learn more about these job titles. (While a list of 10 names is recommended by experts, a list of 6 names is sufficient.)

C. Fill in the Parachute Diagram (appendix B, page 25)

1 This step helps you keep track of the most important factors that matter to you in a fulfilling job or career.

2 Fill in the sections of the Parachute Diagram using information uncovered through exercises in this workbook, the Discovery Exercises in *What Color Is Your Parachute? For Teens*, and/or other career exploration activities completed during the coaching process or career class.

Identifying Jobs You Might Enjoy

Investigate Occupations

Use the Internet to investigate five occupations. List each of the job titles on page 6 and learn what the common work tasks are for each job. Enter that information on the worksheet on page 6.

Continue your research and use what you uncover to complete the chart on the following page. Here are the categories of information to research about each job and then enter on page 7.

> This research is necessary because you want to test your assumptions and the common statements made about this job or line of work.

1 **Official Job Title**

2 **Basic Salary Information**

3 **Transferable Skills Needed/ Used**

4 **Technical Proficiencies Needed**

5 **Education or Training** – What kind? How long is it? How much will it cost?

6 **Typical Work Environment**

7 **Holland Code Matches**

Identifying Jobs You Might Enjoy

Create Job Options -
Investigate 5 Occupations

JOB	JOB TITLE	COMMON WORK TASKS
1		
2		
3		
4		
5		

Identifying Jobs You Might Enjoy

Create Job Options - Investigate 5 Occupations

HOLLAND CODE					
WORK ENVIRON.					
EDUCATION/ TRAINING					
TECH PROFICIENCY					
TRANS. SKILLS					
SALARY					
JOB TITLE					

Identifying Jobs You Might Enjoy

Narrow Down to Top Three Job Titles

Pick 3 of these job titles that still grab your interest after your initial research.

Based on what I learned about the 5 job titles I researched–and from other optional assessments–my **Top Three Job Titles** (for now) are:

Job Title 1: _____

Job Title 2: _____

Job Title 3: _____

My reasons for choosing these titles are (look at your *Parachute Form*
if you have trouble answering this question):

_____

_____

_____

_____

_____

_____

_____

Identifying Jobs You Might Enjoy

Internet Research

Search YouTube and other sites for videos related to your Top Three Job Titles. List links to 3 videos about this line of work, field, job, or industry. Write a sentence about what additional facts you have gathered from the videos.

Job Title #1 _____

Links to videos: **A.** _____   **B.** _____

New facts I learned about this job: _____

_____

_____

Job Title #2 _____

Links to videos: **A.** _____   **B.** _____

New facts I learned about this job: _____

_____

_____

Job Title #3 _____

Links to videos: **A.** _____   **B.** _____

New facts I learned about this job: _____

_____

_____

Identifying Jobs You Might Enjoy

More Internet Research

→ **Identify** 2 professional organizations for each of the three jobs that still interest you and make a record of each URL. The form for capturing this information starts on the next page.

→ **Select** one article or page from the professional organization's website that describes this job in more detail. Copy the URL or link onto the form.

→ **Write** one or two sentences about what additional information you gathered on this job. You can record the bits you like with a + (plus sign) and the bits you didn't like with a – (minus sign)

You Don't:	Have to answer these questions in order
You Do:	Need to answer all questions

DIG A LITTLE DEEPER

While on the websites of professional organizations, find a professional journal for each job you have listed. Read a bit from each publication. To be successful in whatever job you pick, you may need to read blogs, journals or books, attend webinars, or return to school for more studies—so if the subject matter doesn't thrill you, rethink your interest in this job or field.

Why? You need lots more information about yourself and the job market if you want to choose a line of work you will enjoy.

You: Why do I have to make such detailed notes?

Us: Because you just might need to find this information again. The adventure of your life shouldn't be difficult if you learn to work smart. Making records now in case you might need them in a few months, or in a few years, is working smart.

Identifying Jobs You Might Enjoy

Job Title #1 _____

Link to professional organization: _____

Link to professional organization: _____

Link to article: _____

New facts I learned about this job:

_____

_____

Job Title #2 _____

Link to professional organization: _____

Link to professional organization: _____

Link to article: _____

New facts I learned about this job:

_____

_____

Job Title #3 _____

Link to professional organization: _____

Link to professional organization: _____

Link to article: _____

New facts I learned about this job:

_____

_____

Other Internet Resources for Career Information

The Occupational Outlook Handbook   **www.bls.gov/oco**

This website has information such as the field a job is in, working conditions, current employment statistics, earnings, and job outlooks. Click on Job Categories on the right side of the web page to get started.

Department of Labor   **www.dol.gov**

This website includes resources for individuals as well as policy sections and economic and employment statistics. Become familiar with it– you may be coming back to check this website several times in your life!

O*NET Online   **www.onetonline.org**

This website encompasses a free, continually updated database of occupations throughout the US, as well as a variety of career assessment and exploration tools.

Headed2   **www.headed2.com**

This website allows you to identify careers by your 3-letter Holland Code. The Holland Code comes from the Self-Directed-Search® - www.self-directed-search.com.

Eureka   **www.eureka.org**

This site is the online version of a computerized career information system that has been in use for nearly 40 years! As it says on its homepage, EUREKA is a goldmine of career information, and many parts of the website have been translated into Spanish.

(Unlike the other websites listed on this page, access to EUREKA requires a subscription.)

Identifying Jobs You Might Enjoy

Field Research and Informational Interviews

While the term informational interview may be new to you, it's been around a long time in the world of career planning and development. Can you guess what it means? How is it different from a hiring interview?

Conduct 3 informational interviews on each of your Top Three Job Titles. That means you will need to set up at least 9 appointments to talk with people about their work. If you set up 3 interviews a week, you'll complete this task in 3 weeks.

1 Make at least one of these interviews face to face at your interviewee's workplace. You need to become aware of different business environments.

2 If the only way you can talk to someone whose job interests you is through the Internet (Skype, FaceTime or other video chat), do so. But limit yourself to two such interviews. If the people you are talking to are at work, ask if they would show you a bit of their workplace.

3 Eventually, you will develop questions of your own to ask. Until then, use the informational interview questions provided on the following two pages.

4 Remember to fill out a "Capturing the Data from Informational Interviews" worksheet (on pages 16 and 17) for each interview.

> This additional research step is necessary because even information on the web can be limited to a few better known or generalized aspects of the occupation or job. In this exercise, you want to test your assumptions against information from those who do the work that interests you day in and day out.

Identifying Jobs You Might Enjoy

Informational Interview Questions   Page 1

Remember to ask each person the same questions. It will make analyzing their jobs much easier. The questions with ✔ (check marks) next to them are the most basic. We suggest doing practice or warm-up informational interviews prior to interviewing your key contacts.

✔ **1** What do you do? What are the three to five most common tasks you do every day?

✔ **2** How long have you been doing this work?

✔ **3** How did you get into this work?

4 What kind of training and/or education did you need for this job? How much did it cost?

✔ **5** What do you like about your job?

✔ **6** What don't you like about your job?

Identifying Jobs You Might Enjoy

Informational Interview Questions   Page 2

7 What are the main challenges in this field?

8 What do you see happening in this field in the next five to ten years?

9 What is your ultimate career goal?

10 Do you know the starting salary range for this work? What is the salary range for someone with 3 to 6 years of experience?

11 Do you have any additional comments, questions or advice for me if I decide to pursue this career?

12 Can you give me the names of two or three other people who do this (or similar) work?

Identifying Jobs You Might Enjoy

Capturing the Data from Informational Interviews

You want 1 set of worksheets (pages 16-17) for each contact. Please make copies for each person you interview.

Career Goal # _____

Interview # _____

Date of Interview _____

Contact Name:

_____

Contact Title:

_____

Business Phone _____   Mobile/ Home Phone _____

E-mail _____

Skype Name _____

Mailing Address

_____

_____

_____

Information Learned: _____

_____

_____

_____

Identifying Jobs You Might Enjoy

The Job Meter

On a scale of one to ten, rate each job you have investigated. A rating of 8, or more, keeps this job on your list of possibilities. A rating of 7.9, or less, means it's likely this isn't a good job for you.

If you rated a job 7.9 or less, what would have to be different about the job for you to increase its Job Meter rating? Make a detailed list of how you would change the job for the better.

highest

10

9

8

7

6

5

4

3

2

1

lowest

_____

_____

_____

_____

_____

_____

_____

_____

_____

_____

_____

*The Job Meter is the invention of Marty Nemko, PhD. Visit his website, www.martynemko.com for tons of articles on career planning, college planning and other career advice.

Identifying Jobs You Might Enjoy

Bring It All Together

Now you need to combine all the information you have learned about each job on your list. If you leave it scattered throughout several pages, it will be harder for your brain to analyze the information you have compiled and make a decision.

Use the data you've gathered to fill out a two-page Summary Sheet (which starts on the next page) for each of your Top Three Job Titles.

You will need to have 2 additional blank copies of this worksheet in order to complete this exercise.

Identifying Jobs You Might Enjoy

Summary Sheet   Page 1

Job Title # __ : _____

YouTube links: _____

3 Informative Links:

1 _____

2 _____

3 _____

   Comments _____

   _____

   _____

Professional Organizations:

1 _____

2 _____

Article from Professional Organization newsletter, blog or other media:

   Title: _____

   Comments _____

   _____

   _____

Identifying Jobs You Might Enjoy

Summary Sheet
Page 2

Deal makers or deal breakers you learned from informational interviews with people doing this job or a similar one.

_____

_____

_____

Job Meter Rating _____

What would have to be different about this job for you to give it a rating of 9 or 10?

_____

_____

_____

_____

Developing An Action Plan

Next Steps – Career Goal Setting

Collect all the information that you have learned about these 3 job targets in 3 file folders, a 3-ring binder, or in 3 files on your computer. Review what you've learned about your Top Three Job Titles.

Then make a list of your Top Three Job Titles (or enter them in the space provided below), putting your favorite one first. Omit those that don't interest you anymore. The Job Titles that remain on your list are your first career goals.

Top Three Job Titles

Job 1 : _____

Job 2 : _____

Job 3 : _____

During the next 3 to 6 months, your goal is to learn enough about each job you have listed above to choose one as your "Top Pick." Use the worksheet on the following page to get started.

Continue Your Research

During the next 3 to 6 months, your goal is to learn enough about each job you have listed on page 21 to choose one as your "Top Pick." Use the worksheet below to get started.

Steps I need to take to learn more about each of these three jobs:

STEPS	TARGET DATE

Developing An Action Plan

People who can help me (name at least 6):

_____

_____

_____

_____

_____

_____

Target date to contact by:

_____

_____

_____

_____

_____

Decide when you would like to have made a decision about your "Top Pick." Use a calendar and mark this date in your calendar. Set target dates for each of the steps listed on page 22. Jot down the target dates in the column provided and enter them on your personal calendar. Do the same for the target dates to contact people listed above. Refer to pages 22-23 weekly in order to monitor your progress towards reaching your goal. Make adjustments as necessary. Remember, you are not choosing a career or job for life. This is your first, or your next, career move; you are likely to have many more throughout your working life.

Appendix A

Job Categories (used by national & international recruiters)

Accounting	Environmental Protection	Optical
Advertising	Fashion	Payroll/Benefits Administration
Agriculture	Finance	Performance/Fine Arts
Architecture/Design	Food Services	Personal Services
Automotive	Fundraising	Pharmacy
Banking	Gaming	Photography/Videography
Business Development	Government	Planning /Logistics
Career Services	Graphic Arts/Illustration	Politics
Children's Services	Health/Human Services	PR/Public Relations Services
Commercial Arts	Healthcare	Printing and Publishing
Communication	Hotels/Lodging	Project/Program Management
Computer Design	Human Resources	Public Health Administration
Computer Hardware	Industrial Design	Publishing
Computer Software	Information Technology	Real Estate
Construction	Insurance	Retailing
Consulting	Interior design	Sales
Consumer Electronics	Internet	Security
Copywriting/Editing	Journalism	Social Media / Networking
Criminology	Legal	Social Services
Customer Service	Manufacturing Production/ Operations	Sports
Dental	Marketing	Transportation
Digital Media/Online Content	Materials	Travel/Leisure
Economics	Media Planning/Buying	UX / UI/Design
Education	Medical/Health	Veterinary/ Animal Care
Energy/Utilities	Mortgage Professionals	Waste Management
Engineering	Non-profit/Charitable Organizations	Wholesale Trade / Import-Export
Entertainment	Nursing	
Entrepreneurial		

Appendix B

MY PARACHUTE:

This form organizes information about what you want in a job. When it is filled in, use it to guide your research to find a job you will enjoy.

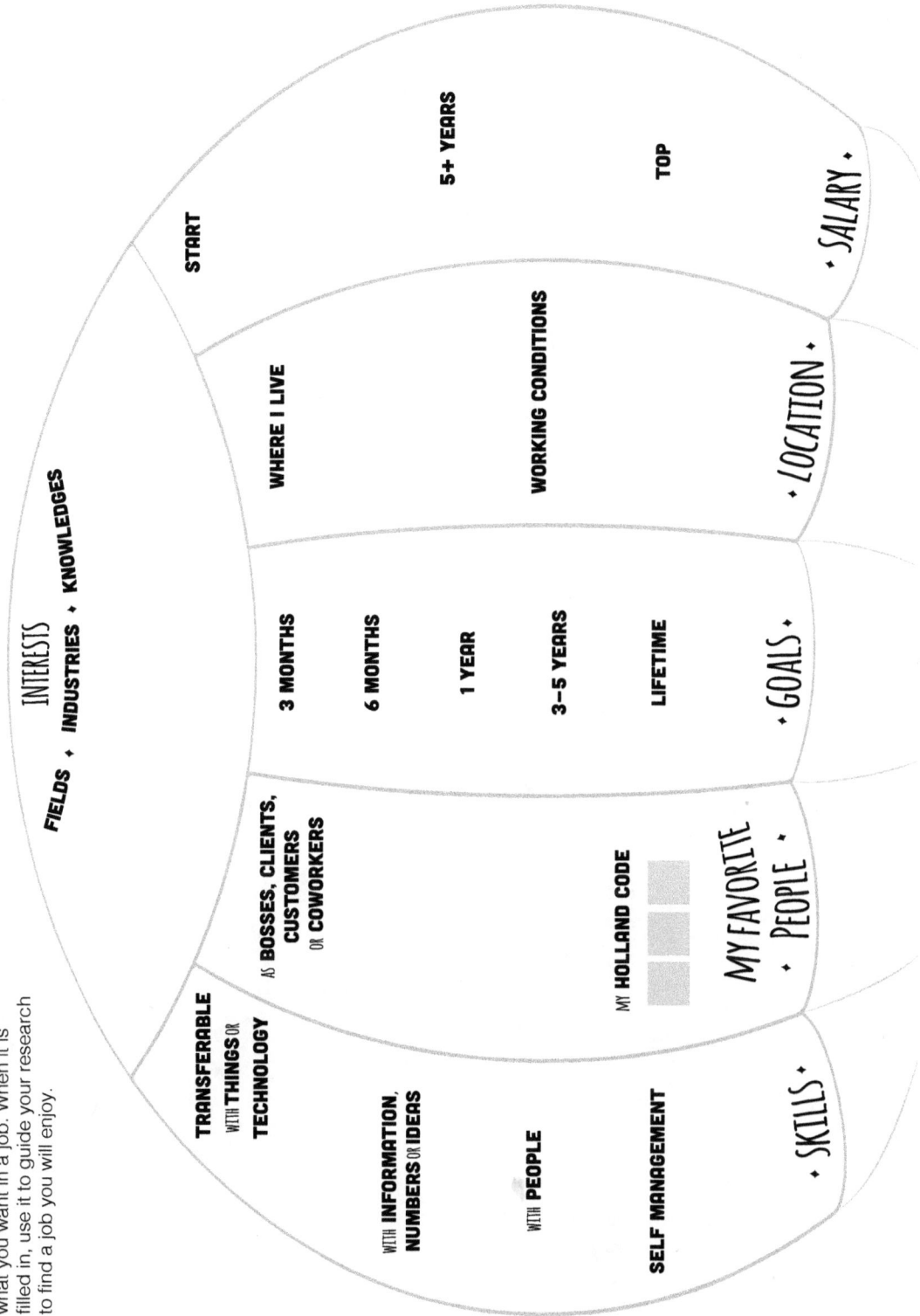

INTERESTS

FIELDS • INDUSTRIES • KNOWLEDGES

START

5+ YEARS

WHERE I LIVE

WORKING CONDITIONS

TOP

• SALARY •

• LOCATION •

3 MONTHS

6 MONTHS

1 YEAR

3–5 YEARS

LIFETIME

• GOALS •

TRANSFERABLE
WITH **THINGS** OR **TECHNOLOGY**

AS **BOSSES, CLIENTS, CUSTOMERS** OR **COWORKERS**

WITH **INFORMATION, NUMBERS** OR **IDEAS**

WITH **PEOPLE**

SELF MANAGEMENT

MY **HOLLAND CODE**

MY FAVORITE • **PEOPLE** •

• SKILLS •

About The Authors

Carol Christen has researched successful transitions from school to work for a decade. She shares that research in this guide and in the 3rd edition of What Color Is Your Parachute For Teens, released April 2015. She is a master teacher of Parachute's empowering career decision making concepts. She ran a federally funded Parachute Program for 17 to 21 year olds and a Job Club for mature workers in an area of high unemployment.

Robin Roman Wright, MA is owner of a Career and ADHD consulting business in Andover, MA. She is a Board Certified Career Coach. She is also a licensed Independent Clinical Social Worker. She is passionate about helping teens and young adults identify their talents and skills as well as discover job opportunities that will be satisfying and rewarding. She has presented to varied audiences on the topic of career planing including the International Career Development Conference, CHADD (Children and Adults with Attention Deficit Hyperactivity Disorder) and the Independent Educational Consultant's Association. Over the last seven years Robin has co-authored an e-zine for parents and teens with Carol Christen.